MEASUREMENT MANIA

Also in the Magical Math series

Magical Math

MEASUREMENT MANIA

Games and Activities
That Make Math Easy and Fun

Lynette Long

John Wiley & Sons, Inc.

New York • Chichester • Weinheim • Brisbane • Singapore • Toronto

This book is printed on acid-free paper. ∞

Copyright © 2001 by Lynette Long. All rights reserved
Illustrations copyright © 2001 by Tina Cash-Walsh.

Published by John Wiley & Sons, Inc.
Published simultaneously in Canada

Design and production by Navta Associates, Inc.

The Publisher and the author have made every reasonable effort to ensure that the experiments and activities in this book are safe when conducted as instructed but assume no responsibility for any damage caused or sustained while performing the experiments or activities in this book. Parents, guardians, and/or teachers should supervise young readers who undertake the experiments and activities in this book.

ISBN 0-471-36980-2

Printed in the United States of America

10 9 8 7 6 5 4 3 2 1

Contents

~~~ I ~~~
THE MAGIC OF MEASUREMENT

Think for a minute of all the things in the world that you can measure:

- the distance to school
- your height
- the volume of liquid in a glass of soda
- your dog's weight
- the temperature outside
- the time it took you to read this list!

In this book you are going to learn about five different forms of measurement—length, volume, weight, temperature, and time—and two different systems of measurement, the English system and the metric system.

Length, such as distance and height, is measured in the English units of inches, feet, yards, and miles, and primarily in the metric units of millimeters, centimeters, meters, and kilometers. Volume is measured in the English units of ounces, cups, quarts, and gallons, and primarily in the metric units of milliliters, liters, and kiloliters. Weight is measured in the English units of ounces, pounds, and tons, and primarily in the metric units of milligrams, grams, kilograms, and metric tons. Temperature is measured in the English units of degrees Fahrenheit and in the metric units of degrees Celsius. Time is measured in seconds, minutes, hours, days, weeks, months, years, decades, centuries, and millennia.

In this book you'll learn to master all the different types and systems of measurement. Try some of the fun activities and soon you'll know how to measure the length of an ant in millimeters, the height of a tree in feet, the volume of your bathtub in ounces, the weight of a spaghetti noodle in grams, and the temperature in your refrigerator in degrees Celsius. How long will it take you to master all the different units of measurement? Will it be seconds, minutes, hours, days, weeks, months, years, or decades? Get started and find out.

~~~ II ~~~

MEASURING LENGTH AND DISTANCE IN ENGLISH AND METRIC UNITS

In the United States we most commonly use what is called the English measurement system (even though the English now use the metric system). The English measurement system uses inches, feet, yards, and miles to measure length. Most of these units of measurement were originally based on parts of the body.

The foot comes from the Romans and is based on the length of a grown man's foot. One foot is divided into 12 inches. King Henry I of England (1068–1135, reigned

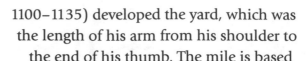

1100–1135) developed the yard, which was the length of his arm from his shoulder to the end of his thumb. The mile is based on the distance covered by a Roman soldier in 1,000 paces. Since people's feet, arms, and paces come in all different lengths, eventually the British standardized these measurements. They cast a standard yard from an iron bar. Copies of this standard yard were made and distributed all over Britain and were the original yardsticks.

Because the English system of measurement is based on lengths of the human body, converting between units can be difficult. You just have to remember there are 12 inches in a foot, 3 feet in a yard, and 1,760 yards or 5,280 feet in a mile.

ENGLISH UNITS OF LENGTH

English Unit	Abbreviation	English Equivalent
inch	in.	
foot	ft.	12 inches
yard	yd.	3 feet (36 inches)
mile	mi.	1,760 yards (5,280 feet)

In the 1790s, members of the French Academy of Sciences developed the metric system, which includes units for measuring length, volume, and weight. The name *metric* comes from the ancient Greek word *metron*, meaning "a measure." If you ever travel outside the United States, it is important to understand the metric system, since metric measurements are the only measurements you'll find. Even in the United States, if you look carefully, you'll find the metric system in use.

The metric system, which is based on the decimal system, uses units of 10 to convert between units. If you can multiply and divide by 10, the metric system is easy to use. The primary units of length in the metric system are millimeters, centimeters, meters, and kilometers.

METRIC UNITS OF LENGTH

Metric Unit	Abbreviation	Metric Equivalent
millimeter	mm	0.1 cm
centimeter	cm	10 mm
decimeter	dm	10 cm
meter	m	100 cm
dekameter	dam	10 m
hectometer	hm	100 m
kilometer	km	1,000 m

In this section, you'll learn how to measure length and distance using English and metric units. You will also measure things using your feet and hands, as well as the standard units of inches, feet, yards, and miles. You'll find out a lot about yourself in this section, including how wide your smile is, how far you can jump, and how long it takes you to run a mile. You'll design a mosaic, create optical illusions, and perhaps measure the tallest building or tree in your neighborhood without climbing an inch. You'll learn what each of the metric units of length represents by measuring a doll, calculating neighborhood distances, making a metric measuring tape, and calculating the distances in kilometers to different parts of the world. You will also learn how to convert distances between English units, between metric units, and between English and metric units. The activities in this section are entertaining and will teach you a lot about distance measurement, so why not get started?

CONVERSIONS FROM METRIC TO ENGLISH EQUIVALENTS

Metric Measurement	English Equivalent
1 mm	0.04 inch
1 cm	0.3937 inch
1 m	39.37 inches or 1 yard 3⅓ inches
1 km	0.62 mile or 1,094 yards

CONVERSIONS FROM ENGLISH TO METRIC EQUIVALENTS

English Measurement	Metric Equivalent
1 inch	2.54 cm
1 foot	0.305 m or 30.5 cm
1 yard	0.914 m
1 mile	1.61 km

Feet First!

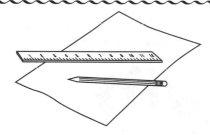

Measure a room using one of the original units of measurement, your foot.

MATERIALS

pencil
paper
ruler

Procedure

1. Copy the following chart on a piece of paper.

2. Write your name in column 1 of the chart. Measure the length of a room by counting how many of your feet it takes to walk across the room. Start at one wall and walk straight across the room, putting one foot in front of

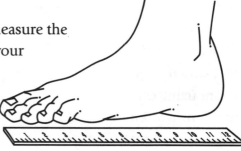

ROOM LENGTH IN "FEET"

Column 1: Self, Friends, and Family	Column 2: Foot Length in Inches	Column 3: Room Length in "Feet"

the other, touching your right heel to your left toe, and your left heel to your right toe. Write the length of the room in "feet" in column 3.

3. Write the name of a friend in column 1. Have your friend measure the length of the room in his or her feet. How many of your friend's feet did it take to measure the room?

4. Put your foot next to your friend's foot. Who has the larger foot? Whose feet did it take more of to measure the room?

5. Measure the length of your foot in inches and write the length in column 2. Multiply the length of your foot by the number of your feet it took to measure the room. The answer is the length of the room in inches.

6. Measure your friend's foot in inches and write the length in column 2. Multiply your friend's foot length by the number of feet it took him or her to measure the room. How do the two measurements compare?

7. Measure the length of the room using other friends' and family members' feet. What is the length in inches of the smallest foot you measured? How many of these feet do you estimate it would take

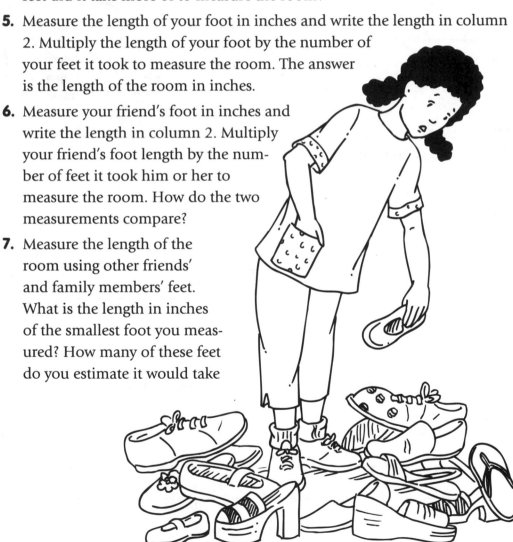

to measure the room? What is the length in inches of the largest foot you measured? How many of these feet do you estimate it would take to measure the room?

BRAIN Stretcher

Go to a shoe store with a ruler and measure the largest size of men's shoes you can find. How long are these shoes in inches? How many feet of this size would it take to measure your room?

SUPER BRAIN Stretcher

Go to a shoe store with a ruler and try to figure out how men's and women's shoes are sized. How many inches different is each size? What is the length of the smallest size in inches? What is the difference between a man's size 9 and a woman's size 9? Find five pairs of women's shoes that are all the same size. Are they all the same length?

Hands Up

Use your hands to measure height.

MATERIALS

pencil
paper
ruler

Procedure

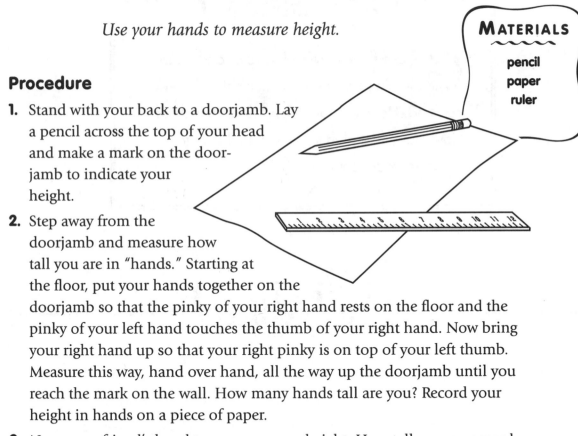

1. Stand with your back to a doorjamb. Lay a pencil across the top of your head and make a mark on the door-jamb to indicate your height.

2. Step away from the doorjamb and measure how tall you are in "hands." Starting at the floor, put your hands together on the doorjamb so that the pinky of your right hand rests on the floor and the pinky of your left hand touches the thumb of your right hand. Now bring your right hand up so that your right pinky is on top of your left thumb. Measure this way, hand over hand, all the way up the doorjamb until you reach the mark on the wall. How many hands tall are you? Record your height in hands on a piece of paper.

3. Now use a friend's hand to measure your height. How tall are you according to your friend's hands?

4. Use a ruler to measure the width of your hand. Put your hand flat on a table and keep your fingers together. Measure the distance across the widest part of your hand from outside your pinky to outside your thumb. Record the width of your hand.

5. Measure other friends' hands. What is the width of the smallest hand? What is the width of the widest hand?

6. Why do you think ancient systems of measurement didn't use feet to measure height?

BRAIN Stretcher

Horses are still measured in hands. One hand is equal to 4 inches (10.2 cm). If the average horse is 15 hands tall from the shoulder to the ground, how tall is the average horse in inches? A large horse is 17 hands tall. How tall is a large horse in inches?

Body Parts

Measure body parts in inches and feet.

MATERIALS

pencil
paper
measuring tape
2 colored pencils
or crayons—1 red,
1 blue

Procedure

1. Copy the following chart on a piece of paper.

BODY PART MEASUREMENTS

	Someone Older	You	Someone Younger
name of person			
"circumference" of (distance around) head			
length of eyebrow			
length of smile			
length of ear			
length of longest strand of hair			
circumference of neck			
length from elbow to wrist			
length of longest finger			
body part of your choice			

2. Find two people to measure. One should be older than you, preferably an adult, and the other should be younger than you.

3. For each person (including yourself), take the measurements of the body parts listed in the chart.

4. With a red pencil or crayon, circle the largest measurement of each type. Which body part is largest?

5. With a blue pencil or crayon, circle the smallest measurement of each type. Which part is smallest?

6. Who has the largest head? Who has the smallest smile? Does the oldest person have the largest of everything? Does the youngest person have the smallest of everything?

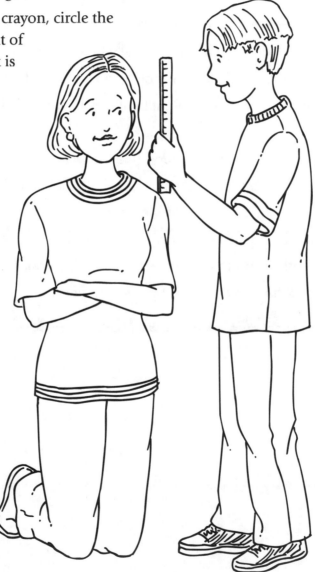

BRAIN Stretcher

1. Find a toddler to measure. Measure the circumference of the toddler's head.

2. Divide the circumference of your head by the circumference of the toddler's head. Record this number.

3. Measure the distance from your belly button to the floor, then measure the distance from the toddler's belly button to the floor.

4. Divide your belly button height by the toddler's belly button height. Record this number.

The two numbers you just found (the answers to steps 2 and 4) are called "ratios." The ratio you got for the belly button height should be larger than the ratio you got for the head circumference. A toddler's body parts are not in the same proportion as an older child's or an adult's. A toddler's head is very large compared with his or her body. It takes years for the rest of the body to catch up with the head.

Jump Start

Measure how far you can jump in feet and inches.

MATERIALS

pencil
paper
yardstick or
measuring tape
chalk

Procedure

1. Copy the following chart on a piece of paper.

2. Try each of the following athletic events three times. Record your distances in inches in the chart.

JUMP START IN INCHES

Event	Trial 1	Trial 2	Trial 3
High Jump			
Standing Broad Jump			
Running Broad Jump			
Longest Step			
Hopping			
Backward Jump			

Event 1: High Jump. Stand facing a wall. With adult permission, reach up and make a chalk mark on the wall as high as you can reach. Now jump up, keeping the hand holding the chalk fully extended. At the top of your

jump, make a chalk mark on the wall. Measure the distance between the two chalk marks. This is how high you can jump.

Event 2: Standing Broad Jump. Draw a chalkline on a sidewalk. Stand with the toes of both feet touching the line. Then jump as far as you can. Stay in place where you landed and make a chalk mark behind the heel that is closest to the chalkline. Measure the distance from the chalkline to the chalk mark. This is how far you can jump when standing.

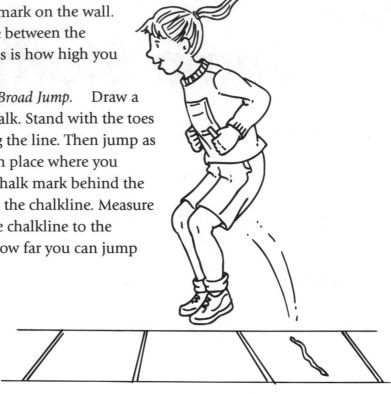

Event 3: Running Broad Jump. Run down the sidewalk toward the chalkline and jump just before you get to the line. (Come as close to the line as you can without stepping on it.) Stay where you landed and make a chalk mark behind the heel that is closest to the chalkline. Measure the distance from the chalkline to the chalk mark. This is how far you can jump when running.

Event 4: Longest Step. Stand with the chalkline behind the heel of one foot. Take the longest step you can with your other foot and make a chalk mark behind the heel of the second foot. Measure the distance from the chalkline to the chalk mark to get the length of your longest step.

Event 5: Hopping. Stand on one foot behind the chalkline and hop forward. Make a chalk mark behind the heel of your hopping foot. Measure the distance between the chalkline and the chalk mark to get your hopping distance.

Event 6: Backward Jump.   Stand with the chalkline behind the heels of both feet and jump backward as far as you can. Make a chalk mark at the tip of your toes and measure the distance between the chalkline and the chalk mark. This is how far you can jump backward.

3. Make a Personal Best Distances chart like the one shown. Record your best distance in each event in inches and in feet and inches. (See the Tips and Tricks box for help in converting inches to feet and inches.) Does writing a measurement one way rather than another way make it seem longer?

PERSONAL BEST DISTANCES

Event	Distance in Inches	Distance in Feet and Inches
High Jump		
Standing Broad Jump		
Running Broad Jump		
Longest Step		
Hopping		
Backward Jump		

Tips and Tricks

To convert a measurement from inches to feet and inches, divide the number of inches by 12. Write the answer in feet and leave the "remainder" R (the number left over) in inches.

For example, to convert 52 inches to feet and inches:

$52 \div 12 = 4 \text{ R}4$

52 inches = 4 feet 4 inches

Add a fifth and sixth column to your Jump Start in Inches chart. Label column 5 "Difference." For each event, subtract your worst (shortest) distance from your best distance and write the "difference" (subtraction answer) in column 5. In which event is the difference greatest? In which event is the difference smallest?

Label column 6 "Percent." For each event, take the difference from column 5 and divide it by the worst distance in that row, using a calculator if necessary. Multiply the quotient (division answer) by 100. Then write the "product" (multiplication answer) in column 6. These numbers show your percentage of improvement. In which event did you make the greatest improvement?

A Simple Ruler

Make your own 6-inch ruler to measure things.

MATERIALS

pencil

two 4-by-6-inch
index cards

books and other
things to measure

ruler

Procedure

1. Fold an index card in half lengthwise. Make a
mark on the edge of the card at the fold line
and label the mark "2 inches."

2. Fold the index card in half lengthwise again. You've now
divided the card into four sections that are each 1-inch wide.
Mark the folds and label them "1 inch" and "3 inches."

3. Use the labeled card to mark a second index
card in 1-inch segments on the long edge.
Label the inches. This second card is your 6-
inch ruler.

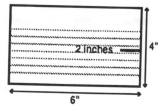

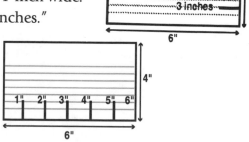

19

4. Now you are ready to measure anything in your house. Try measuring the length and width of a book using your index card ruler. Check your measurements using a real ruler. If the book or other object is longer than your index card ruler, just put your finger at the 6-inch end of the index card ruler and move the index card so that its starting point is where your finger rests. Multiply the length of your index card ruler by the number of times you had to use it to measure the object.

5. What else can you measure with your index card ruler?

BRAIN Stretcher

How can you use a 4-by-6-inch index card and a piece of white ribbon to make a tape measure?

A Tall Order

Measure the height of tall outdoor objects on a sunny day using their shadows and a yardstick.

MATERIALS

2 yardsticks (or 1 yardstick and 1 ruler)

pencil

paper

calculator

Procedure

1. Find something outside that is too tall for you to measure easily, such as your house, a tree, or a flagpole.

2. Hold a yardstick perpendicular to the ground and use the second yardstick (or a ruler) to measure the length of the shadow the yardstick casts in inches. Record this length on a piece of paper.

3. Now measure and record the length of the shadow of the tall object you want to measure.

4. Divide the length of the shadow of the yardstick by the length of the yardstick, using a calculator if necessary. This ratio is equal to the length of the shadow of the tall object divided by the one thing you don't know, the height of the tall object. The formula looks like this:

$$\frac{\text{length of shadow of yardstick}}{\text{length of yardstick}} = \frac{\text{length of shadow of tall object}}{\text{height of tall object}}$$

For example, if your yardstick casts a 12-inch shadow and the shadow of a tree you measured is 15 yards long, here's how to calculate the height of the tree:

$$\frac{12 \text{ inches}}{36 \text{ inches}} = \frac{15 \text{ yards}}{\text{height of tree}}$$

Now "cross multiply." To do this, multiply each "numerator" (the value above the line of a fraction) by the "denominator" (the value below the line) on the opposite side of the problem, as follows:

$12 \times \text{height of tree} = 15 \times 36$
$12 \times \text{height of tree} = 540$

Now take the problem $12 \times$ height of tree $= 540$ and divide both sides by 12:

$12 \div 12 = 1$
$540 \div 12 = 45$

The tree is 45 yards tall. (Since the shadow of the tree is measured in yards, the height of the tree is also in yards.)

The Magnificent Mile

How quickly can you run a mile?

MATERIALS

car and driver
running shoes or
sneakers
stopwatch
pencil
paper
calculator

Procedure

1. While the car is parked, take a look at the dashboard. Have the driver point out the speedometer and the odometer. The speedometer indicates how fast the car is going in miles per hour. The odometer indicates how many miles the car has been driven, to the nearest tenth of a mile. Under the odometer is the trip odometer. The trip odometer can be reset to zero so you can measure the distance traveled in a trip. Odometers and trip odometers measure miles based on a ratio of the circumference of the car's wheels to the number of times the wheels turn. If a wheel has a circumference of 8 feet, then 660 turns of the wheel equals 1 mile (since there are 5,280 feet in a mile).

2. Ask the driver to set the trip odometer to zero.

3. Now try to find a route around your neighborhood that is exactly 1 mile. The route should start and end at the same point, and it should stick to quiet roads with sidewalks, not highways or busy streets. If the first route you picked is too long or too short, ask the driver to drive back to the starting point, set the trip odometer to zero, and try again.

4. Now put on your running shoes or sneakers and run your 1-mile route. Be sure to stay on the sidewalk. Ask the driver to time how long it takes you to run a mile. Record your time on a piece of paper.

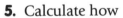

5. Calculate how fast you ran in miles per hour using the formula distance/time = speed and a calculator if necessary. First, convert your time from minutes to hours by dividing your time in minutes by 60 (since there are 60 minutes in 1 hour). Next, divide the distance (which is 1 mile) by the time in hours to determine your speed in miles per hour. For example, if it takes you 20 minutes to run a mile, it takes you 20/60 hour. "Reduce" (simplify to lower terms) the fraction 20/60 to get 1/3. Now use the formula distance/time = speed to calculate your speed. The problem reads: (1 mile)/(1/3 hour) = speed. Divide the "dividend," 1 mile, by the "divisor," 1/3 hour. The divisor is a fraction, so "invert" it (turn it upside down) and multiply the dividend by the inverted divisor. Now the problem reads: $1 \times 3/1 = 3$. So, if it takes you 20 minutes to run a mile, you can run 3 miles per hour.

6. Run your course again. How long did it take you to run a mile on your second try? How many miles per hour did you run?

BRAIN Stretchers

1. The fastest people in the world can run a mile in about 4 minutes. How many miles per hour do these people run? Ride in a car at this same speed. Does it seem fast or slow?

2. If it takes you 21 minutes to run 3 miles, how many miles per hour are you running? First figure out how long it took you to run 1 mile; then calculate your speed in miles per hour.

3. If you can run a mile in 8 minutes 30 seconds, how many miles per hour are you running? Change 8 minutes 30 seconds to 8.5 minutes. Divide 8.5 by 60, which is your time in hours. Now that you know your time, calculate your speed.

Area Mosaic

"Area" is the measurement of a flat surface within a boundary of lines. Area is measured in square units. Practice measuring area by making a mosaic.

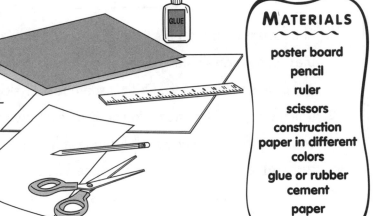

MATERIALS

poster board
pencil
ruler
scissors
construction paper in different colors
glue or rubber cement
paper

Procedure

1. On a piece of poster board, draw a square that is 1 foot long and 1 foot wide. This is 1 square foot.

2. Use your pencil and ruler to draw vertical lines inside this square that are 1 inch apart, starting 1 inch from either side of the square. There should be 12 columns.

3. Now draw horizontal lines 1 inch apart. There should be 144 little squares inside the large square. The square is 12 inches by 12 inches, which means it is 12 × 12 or 144 square inches.

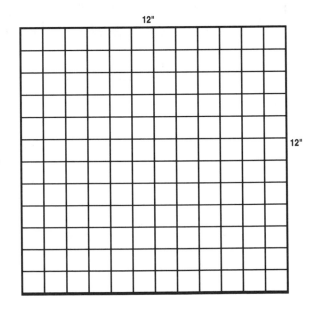

12"

12"

4. Cut pieces of different colored construction paper into 1-inch squares. You'll need at least 144 squares altogether.

5. Glue these 1-inch squares of colored construction paper on the piece of poster board in a pattern or picture of your own design. This is called a "mosaic."

6. Copy the following chart on a piece of paper.

MOSAIC COLORS

Color	Number of Squares	Fraction of Color	Percentage of Color

7. List each color in your mosaic in column 1 of the chart.

8. Count the number of squares of each color you used. Write this number in column 2.

9. Divide the number of squares in column 2 by 144. Write this number in column 3. This is the fraction of each color you used in your mosaic.

10. Change the fraction of color to a decimal. Multiply this decimal by 100. Write this number in column 4. This is the percentage of each color you used in your mosaic.

11. Which color did you use the most of? The least? Have a friend estimate the percentage of each color just by looking at the mosaic. How accurate is the estimate?

1. How many square feet are there in a square yard? Use a piece of chalk and a yardstick to draw a square yard on the sidewalk. Divide this square yard into square feet. Count the squares. There are 9 square feet in 1 square yard.

2. How many square yards are there in a square mile? Multiply the number of yards in a mile by itself. What is $1,760 \times 1,760$?

Optical Illusions

Learn about area while creating "optical illusions,"
images that are misleading.

MATERIALS

five 4-by-6-inch
index cards

scissors

glue

2 pieces of con-
struction paper

Procedure

1. Fold five 4-by-6 index
   cards in half so that the short
   sides are together, then cut the
   cards in half along the fold line.

2. Glue five half cards on each piece of
   construction paper. Arrange the half cards on each piece of paper in different patterns, so that different amounts of paper seem to show in each
   pattern. Use exactly five half cards on each sheet of paper and don't over-
   lap the cards.

3. Cut out the pieces of construction paper covered by half cards in such a
   way that the remaining construction paper is still in one piece. These are
   your optical illusions. Although each optical illusion looks different, they
   both have the same area.

4. Show your optical illusions to a friend. Ask him or her which one is big-
   ger. Can your friend tell that they are really all the same size?

Figure out the area of your optical illusions.

1. Find the area of the entire piece of construction paper. If the construction paper is 11 by 14 inches, each sheet then is 11 × 14, or 154 square inches.
2. Find the area of each half card. The index cards started out as 4 by 6 inches and you cut them in half with the short sides together, so the total area of each half card is 4 × 3, or 12 square inches.
3. Multiply the number of half cards you used in each optical illusion by 12 square inches. Since you used five half cards, you covered 5 × 12, or 60 square inches, of each piece of construction paper.
4. Subtract the total area of the half cards from the total area of the construction paper to find the visible area of the construction paper in each optical illusion: 154 square inches – 60 square inches = 94 square inches.

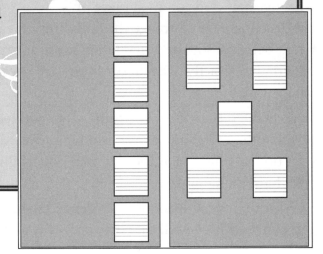

Room Redecorating

Create a fantasy bedroom and learn all about measurement.

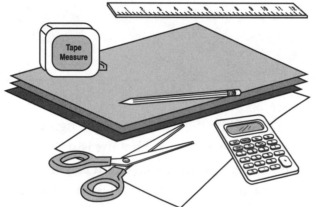

MATERIALS

metal tape measure

pencil

paper

several pieces of construction paper in different colors

ruler

scissors

Procedure

1. Measure the length and width of your room with a tape measure. Record the measurements on a piece of paper.

2. On a white piece of construction paper, draw a bird's-eye view of your room to scale. For the scale, let 1 inch of your drawing represent 1 foot of your room. If your room is 12 feet long and 10 feet wide, use a ruler to draw a rectangle that is 12 by 10 inches. Use pencil lines to indicate on your drawing where the doors and windows are.

3. Measure your furniture and cut out models from different colored pieces of construction paper in the same scale as your model room. If your bed is 3 feet wide and 6 feet long, cut out a 3-by-6-inch piece of colored construction paper. Cut out pieces of construction paper to represent the other objects in your room. Arrange the paper furniture in your model room in different ways to see all the possibilities.

4. Pretend you are going to get new blinds or curtains. In order to buy blinds or curtains you have to know the height and width of each window in inches. Measure the height and width of your windows using a tape measure.

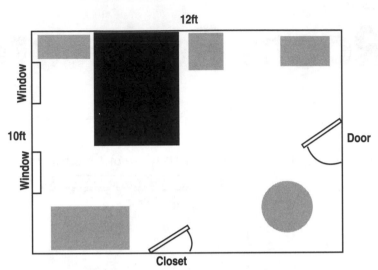

Bird's-eye view of bedroom

5. Maybe you'd like a new wall-to-wall carpet. Carpet is sold by the square yard. To figure out how many square yards of carpet you would need, first measure the length and width of your room in feet. Multiply the length of your room by the width to find the area of the floor in square feet. Divide this number by 9 to find the area in square yards, using a calculator if necessary. If your room is 12 feet long and 10 feet wide, the area of your room is 12 × 10 or 120 square feet. When you divide 120 by 9, you get 13.3, the area of your room in square yards. You would need at least 14 square yards of carpet.

6. How about some new paint for the walls? Paint is sold according to how many square feet of wall and ceiling space you want to cover. To determine the amount of wall and ceiling space in your room, calculate the area of each wall of your room and the area of the ceiling, and add them together. To find the area of one wall in square feet, multiply the length of the wall by the height of the ceiling. (Use a tape measure to find the height of your ceiling.) In a room that is 12 by 10 feet with 8-foot-high ceilings, the total area is calculated as follows:

Area of wall 1: 10 × 8 = 80 square feet
Area of wall 2: 10 × 8 = 80 square feet

Area of wall 3: $12 \times 8 = 96$ square feet

Area of wall 4: $12 \times 8 = 96$ square feet

Area of ceiling: $10 \times 12 = 120$ square feet

Total area = 472 square feet

You would you need enough paint to cover approximately 500 square feet.

BRAIN Stretcher

How would you find the area of your room if it had an unusual shape? If your room had an L shape and the dimensions shown, how would you calculate its area?

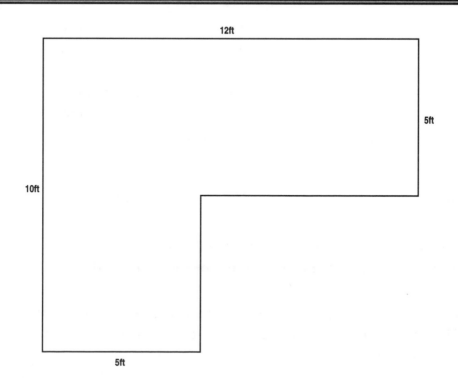

Conversion Cards

Practice converting between different English units of length.

Game Preparation

1. Write "inches" on each of four index cards. Do the same for "feet," "yards," and "miles," so that there are 16 cards altogether. On the back of each card, write "UM," which stands for unit of measurement.

2. Write one of the following expressions on each of 16 other index cards:

6 inches	2 feet	1 yard	¹/₂ mile
24 inches	10 feet	3 yards	1 mile
72 inches	30 feet	10 yards	2 miles
108 inches	42 feet	100 yards	10 miles

Write "Expression" on the back of each of these cards.

Game Rules

1. Shuffle all 32 cards and spread them on the table so that the "UM" and "Expression" sides are face up.

2. Each player gets a calculator and a pencil and paper.

3. Both players simultaneously draw two cards, one UM card and one Expression card.

4. Both players change the expression on their Expression card to the units on their UM card. Players can use their calculators, the Tips and Tricks box, and a pencil and paper.

34

5. The first player to finish shouts, "Done!"

6. The other player stops working and checks the answer of the player who is finished. If the player's answer is correct, he or she wins all four cards. If the answer is incorrect, the other player wins the cards.

7. When all the cards have been played, the player with the most cards wins the game.

SUPER CONVERSION CARDS

Add eight more UM cards to the deck. Write "millimeters" on two cards, "centimeters" on two, "meters" on two, and "kilometers" on two. Add eight more Expression cards to the deck and write one of the following expressions on each:

1 mm	1 cm	1 m	1 km
500 mm	250 cm	20 m	5 km

Shuffle all 48 cards. Play is the same as for Conversion Cards, except players convert also between English and metric units of measurement. Players can also use the conversion tables on page 6.

Tips and Tricks

To convert inches
  to feet divide by 12
  to yards divide by 36
  to miles divide by 63,360

To convert feet
  to inches multiply by 12
  to yards divide by 3
  to miles divide by 5,280

To convert yards
  to inches multiply by 36
  to feet multiply by 3
  to miles divide by 1,760

To convert miles
  to inches multiply by 63,360
  to feet multiply by 5,280
  to yards multiply by 1,760

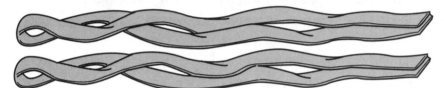

Metric Measuring Tape

Learn about metric measurements by making a metric measuring tape.

MATERIALS

long piece of
ribbon (about 4
yards)

yardstick or ruler

marker

Procedure

1. Lay a long piece of ribbon on a table. Place a yardstick on top of the ribbon and make a mark at the 36-inch end of the yardstick. This mark is one yardstick length. If you are using a ruler, measure three ruler lengths along the ribbon and make a mark at the end of the third ruler length.

2. Place the beginning of the yardstick or ruler on the mark you made in step 1 and measure $3\frac{1}{3}$ more inches along your ribbon. Make a mark here and cut the ribbon on this mark. Your ribbon is now 1 m long. A meter is also 100 cm. Write a 100 at the right end of the ribbon.

3. Fold the ribbon in half. Mark the ribbon at the fold and write a 50 at this point. This is the 50-cm mark.

4. Fold the ribbon in half from the left end to the 50-cm mark. Mark the fold and write a 25 at this mark. Then fold the ribbon in half from the 50-cm mark to the right end, mark the fold, and write a 75 at this mark. The ribbon is now divided into 25-cm sections.

5. Fold each 25-cm section into five equal sections and make a mark at each fold. This divides the ribbon into 5-cm sections. Mark each section in order: 5, 10, 15, 20, and so on, all the way up to 95.

6. Use your metric measuring tape to measure various objects.

BRAIN Stretcher

Is a meter longer or shorter than a yard? If something is 10 yards long, approximately how many meters is it? Is it more than 10 m, less than 10 m, or exactly 10 m?

SUPER BRAIN Stretchers

1. Change 10 yards to meters. There are 36 inches in a yard and 39.37 inches in a meter. Divide 36 by 39.37 to get 0.914. One yard is equal to 0.914 m. So 10 yards is equal to 10 × 0.914 or 9.14 m.

2. Change 10 m to yards. Divide 39.37 by 36. The result, 1.094, is the number of yards in a meter. Multiply 10 by 1.094 to get 10.94. So 10 m is equal to 10.94 yards.

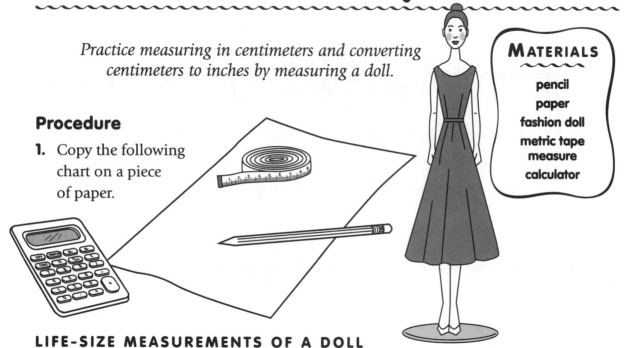

13

Little Dolls, Real People

Practice measuring in centimeters and converting centimeters to inches by measuring a doll.

MATERIALS

pencil
paper
fashion doll
metric tape
measure
calculator

Procedure

1. Copy the following chart on a piece of paper.

LIFE-SIZE MEASUREMENTS OF A DOLL

Parts of Doll	Doll's Measurements in Centimeters	Life-Size Measurements in Centimeters	Life-Size Measurements in Inches
height			
arm length			
waist size			
chest size			
hip size			
leg length			
foot size			

2. Find a fashion doll, such as a Barbie doll. Use a metric tape measure to take the following doll measurements in centimeters: height, arm length, waist size, chest size, hip size, leg length, and foot size. Write these measurements in column 2 of the chart.

3. Divide 168 cm, which is the height of the average woman, by the doll's height, using a calculator if you need to. The result is how many times you must multiply the doll's height to get the height of an average-size woman.

4. Multiply each of the doll's measurements by the number you found in step 3. These are what the doll's measurements would be in centimeters if she were life-size. Write the life-size measurements in centimeters in column 3.

5. Multiply the numbers in column 3 by 0.39 to convert from centimeters to inches. Write the life-size measurements in inches in column 4.

6. When you have filled in the chart, look at the measurements in column 4. Do they seem realistic? Compare these measurements to those of a woman you know who is of average height and weight.

14

Neighborhood Distances

Use your bicycle to measure long outdoor distances.

MATERIALS

pencil
paper
metric
measuring tape
bicycle
chalk
calculator

Procedure

1. Copy the following chart on a piece of paper.

NEIGHBORHOOD DISTANCES

Parts of Neighborhood	Number of Wheel Revolutions	Distance in Centimeters	Distance in Meters	Distance in Kilometers
length of house or apartment building				
length of front yard				
length of backyard				
length of driveway				
distance to school				
distance to friend's house				
distance to park or playground				

2. Use a metric measuring tape to measure the circumference of the front tire of your bicycle in centimeters. Wrap your measuring tape all the way around the part of the tire that touches the ground to get an accurate measurement. Record this measurement on a piece of paper.

3. Make a thick chalk mark on the side wall of the tire. Turn the wheel of the tire so that the chalk mark is straight up and exactly in line with the frame of the bike.

4. As you slowly ride your bike to measure the lengths and distances of your neighborhood listed in column 1 of the chart, have a friend count the

number of revolutions the front tire of the bike makes. (At each revolution, your friend will see the chalk mark come back up to its original position.) Write the number of wheel revolutions in column 2.

5. Multiply the number of revolutions in column 1 by the circumference of the front tire, using a calculator if necessary. This is the distance you traveled in centimeters. Write this distance in column 3.

6. Divide the distance in column 3 by 100. This is the distance you traveled in meters. Write this distance in column 4.

7. Divide the distance in column 4 by 1,000. This is the distance you traveled in kilometers. Write this distance in column 5.

BRAIN Stretcher

Convert the distances you found from metric to English units. Multiply the distance in column 4 (meters) by 1.09 to get the distance you traveled in yards. Multiply the distance in column 5 (kilometers) by 0.62 to get the distance you traveled in miles.

Kilometer Vacations

Take an imaginary vacation and practice converting from miles to kilometers.

Procedure

1. Make a list of the places in the United States you would like to visit. Maybe you would like to go to New York City to climb to the top of the Statue of Liberty, or perhaps you want to watch Old Faithful erupt at Yellowstone National Park, or maybe you want to swim in the Atlantic Ocean at Miami Beach.

2. Use an atlas to find the distances in miles from your house to the places on your list. Write the distances next to the place-names on your list.

3. Use a calculator to multiply each of the distances by 1.61. The results are the distances to your favorite places in kilometers.

4. On a piece of poster board use a yardstick (meterstick) to draw big arrows that are about 4 inches (10 cm) wide and 18 inches (30 cm) long. You will need one arrow for each place on your list. Cut out the arrows.

5. On each of the arrows, write the name of one of the places you want to visit. Below the place-name, write the distance in both miles and kilometers. Use the abbreviation *mi.* for miles and *km* for kilometers.

6. With adult permission, tape the arrows to walls in your house, using the atlas and a compass to point each arrow in the correct direction.

BRAIN Stretcher

The next time you go on a car trip, take a calculator with you and convert every road sign from miles to kilometers.

When you see a sign that says, for example, COLUMBUS 36 MILES, multiply 36 by 1.61 to find the distance to Columbus in kilometers.

Dancing Decimal Points

Practice converting from one metric unit to another.

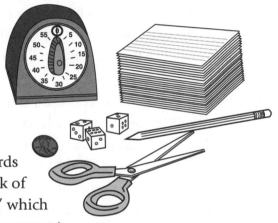

MATERIALS

pencil

27 index cards

scissors

3 dice

penny

3-minute egg
timer or other
timer

2 or more players

Game Preparation

1. Write "kilometer" on each of three index cards. Do the same for "meter," "centimeter," and "millimeter," so that there are 12 cards altogether. On the back of each card, write "UM," which stands for unit of measurement.

2. Cut 15 other index cards in half to make 30 minicards.

3. Take 12 of the minicards and write a zero on each card.

4. Take the other 18 minicards and divide them into six groups of three cards each. Write a 1 on each card in the first group, a 2 on each card in the second group, a 3 on each card in the third group, a 4 on each card in the fourth group, a 5 on each card in the fifth group, and a 6 on each card in the sixth group.

Game Rules

1. Spread the minicards faceup on the table. Shuffle the UM cards and place them in a stack on the table so that the UM side is faceup.

2. Player 1 rolls three dice, then finds the three minicards that match the numbers on the dice and places them in a row. Player 1 places a penny to the right of the third number to represent a decimal point. For example, if the player rolls a 6, a 4, and a 2, he or she places the 6, 4, and 2 minicards in a row, with a penny to the right of the 2 card.

3. Player 1 turns the top UM card over. This is the unit of measurement the three minicards are first expressed in. If the UM card is a centimeter card, the minicards express 642 cm.

4. Player 1 sets the timer. The player has 3 minutes to convert the expression to as many different units of measurement as he or she can by moving the decimal point (penny). Zeros can be added as necessary, using the 0 (zero) minicards. The player can use the Tips and Tricks box for help in converting between units.

5. Player 1 turns the next UM card over, and places it on top of the previous UM card. If the UM card is a millimeter card, the player quickly places a 0 (zero) card to the right of the 2 card and moves the penny to the right of the 0 (zero) card. The minicards now express 6,420 mm. When everyone agrees that the answer is correct, player 1 turns the next UM card over and converts the expression again. If the UM card is a meter card, the player quickly moves the penny to the right of the 6 card. The cards now express 6.420 m.

6. When the 3 minutes are up, player 1 earns 1 point for each UM card played correctly. If the player plays all 12 cards correctly in 3 minutes, he or she earns 15 points.

7. All the UM cards are shuffled and placed facedown in a stack on the table.

8. Player 2 takes a turn. The first player to earn 25 points is the winner.

SUPER DANCING DECIMAL POINTS

Add more UM cards to your deck, three each in the units decimeter (dm), decameter (dam), and hectometer (hm). (See Tips and Tricks box for information on their values.) Or make a whole new set of UM cards. Choose milliliter, centiliter, liter, and kiloliter, or choose milligram, centigram, gram, and kilogram. Converting between units is the same process as for millimeters, centimeters, meters, and kilometers.

Tips and Tricks

To convert millimeters
- to centimeters divide by 10
- to meters divide by 1,000
- to kilometers divide by 1,000,000

To convert centimeters
- to millimeters multiply by 10
- to meters divide by 1,000
- to kilometers divide by 100,000

To convert meters
- to centimeters multiply by 100
- to millimeters multiply by 1,000
- to kilometers divide by 1,000

To convert kilometers
- to meters multiply by 1,000
- to centimeters multiply by 100,000
- to millimeters multiply by 1,000,000

Each greater metric unit of measurement is 10 times larger than the one before it: 1,000,000 mm = 100,000 cm = 10,000 dm = 1,000 m = 100 dam = 10 hm = 1 km. In order to remember the sequence of the metric units of measurement, memorize this sentence: "My Cute Dog Marches Down His Kennel." The first letters of the words are the first letters of the metric units, from smallest to largest.

17 Metric-English Frenzy

Learn the relative values of metric and English measurements.

MATERIALS

2 to 3 pencils
17 index cards
calculator
several pieces of paper
2 to 3 players

Game Preparation

Write one of the following distances on each of 17 index cards.

1 m	10 m	1 yard	10 yards
1 cm	10 cm	1 foot	5 feet
1 km	10 km	1 inch	5 inches
1 mm		1 mile	10 miles

the distance from Earth to the Moon
the distance from Earth to the Sun

Game Rules

1. Shuffle the cards and deal each player five cards.

2. Each player places his or her cards in a row facedown on the table.

3. On the count of three, all players turn their cards over and put them in order from smallest to largest, reading from left to right. If players are not sure which measurements are largest, they can convert the expressions on the cards to the same units using the conversion tables on page 6, a calculator, and a pencil and paper. The first player who puts his or her cards in the correct order wins the round.

4. Collect all the cards, shuffle them, and deal each player another five cards. The first player to win three rounds wins the game.

SUPER METRIC-ENGLISH FRENZY

Write numerical facts about common items or animals on index cards, such as the height of an elephant, the width of a book, the length of your bedroom, and the diameter of a saucer. Add these cards to the deck, shuffle the cards, deal each player five cards, and see who is the first to place his or her cards in order from smallest to largest.

MEASURING VOLUME IN ENGLISH AND METRIC UNITS

"Volume" is the amount of space occupied by something. In most kitchens in the United States, you are likely to find lots of implements for measuring English units of volume, such as teaspoons, tablespoons, ounces, and cups. If you look in the refrigerator, you might also find a pint of half-and-half, a quart of orange juice, and a gallon of milk. In the English system of measuring volume, 8 ounces make 1 cup, 2 cups make 1 pint, 2 pints

make 1 quart, and 4 quarts make 1 gallon. (Because the word *ounce* is also used to indicate weight in the English system, the ounces used to measure volume are often called "fluid ounces.")

COMMON ENGLISH UNITS OF VOLUME

English Unit	Abbreviation	English Equivalent
teaspoon	tsp.	⅓ tablespoon
tablespoon	tb.	1⁄16 cup, or ½ ounce
cup	c.	8 ounces
pint	pt.	2 cups
quart	qt.	2 pints
gallon	gal.	4 quarts

If you were in a kitchen in another part of the world, however, you would find a lot of metric volume measurements. You would buy a liter of milk or maybe 250 ml of cream. The most commonly used units of volume in the metric system are milliliters, liters, and kiloliters. A liter is defined as the volume occupied by 1 kg of pure water at 4°C. A milliliter is 0.001 l, and a kiloliter is 1,000 l.

COMMON METRIC UNITS OF VOLUME

Metric Unit	Abbreviation	Metric Equivalent
milliliter	ml	0.1 cl
centiliter	cl	10 ml
deciliter	dl	100 ml
liter	l	1,000 ml
kiloliter	kl	1,000 l

In this section, you'll learn about volume using English and metric units. You will figure out how many tablespoons are in 1 cup, learn how to make a square cup, and figure out multiples of given numbers. You'll learn how to recognize a milliliter, make a liter container, and figure out the best value at the grocery store no matter what units of measurement are used. You will also learn how to convert volume measurements between English units, between metric units, and between English and metric units.

CONVERSIONS FROM METRIC TO ENGLISH EQUIVALENTS

Metric Measurement	English Equivalent
1 ml	0.0338 ounce
1 cl	0.338 ounce
1 dl	0.21 pint
1 l	1.057 quarts

CONVERSIONS FROM ENGLISH TO METRIC EQUIVALENTS

English Measurement	Metric Equivalent
1 teaspoon	5 ml
1 tablespoon	15 ml
1 ounce	29.573 ml
1 pint	0.473 l
1 quart	0.946 l
1 gallon	3.785 l

Spoons Abound

Learn the relationship between teaspoons, tablespoons, and cups.

MATERIALS

teaspoon
water
tablespoon
sugar
butter knife
1-cup measuring cup
1 package instant oatmeal

Procedure

1. Fill a teaspoon with water. Pour it into an empty tablespoon. Keep pouring teaspoons of water into the tablespoon until it is full. How many teaspoons does it take to fill 1 tablespoon?

2. Dry both spoons carefully. Measure 1 level tablespoon using heaping teaspoons of sugar. In a heaping spoonful, the material being measured is piled higher than the rim of the spoon, but in a level spoonful, the material does not extend higher than the rim of the spoon. Use the straight edge of a butter knife to level the sugar in the spoon. To determine the number of heaping teaspoons in 1 level tablespoon, try not to spill any sugar over the rim of the spoon as you level the sugar. How many heaping teaspoons equal 1 level tablespoon?

3. Empty the tablespoon, then fill it with level teaspoons of sugar. What is the difference between the number of teaspoons it takes to make a tablespoon when you use level teaspoons of sugar and when you use heaping teaspoons of sugar?

4. Fill the tablespoon with water. Pour the water into an empty measuring cup. Keep filling the cup with tablespoons of water. How many tablespoons of water equal exactly 1 cup of water?

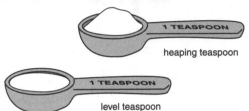

heaping teaspoon

level teaspoon

5. Empty the cup and dry it carefully. Fill the cup with level tablespoons of sugar. How many level tablespoons of sugar equal 1 cup of sugar?

6. Fill the cup with heaping tablespoons of sugar. How many heaping tablespoons equal 1 cup?

7. Empty the cup, and repeat step 6. How many heaping tablespoons of sugar did it take to fill the cup this time? Did it take the same number of spoonfuls? One heaping tablespoon of sugar may not be equal to another heaping tablespoon of sugar. Recipes usually call for level teaspoons and tablespoons since one level spoonful is more likely equal to another level spoonful than two heaping spoonfuls are equal to each other.

8. Prepare a package of instant oatmeal, but instead of using a measuring cup to measure the water, use just teaspoons and tablespoons. How many teaspoons or tablespoons of water do you have to add?

BRAIN Stretcher

Open a cookbook and find a recipe that uses cups. Convert the cups entirely to tablespoons. Now convert the tablespoons to teaspoons.

Measuring Cup

Make your own English measuring cup.

MATERIALS

12-oz. can of soda

5 glasses that are exactly the same size

1 large glass (at least 12-ounce capacity)

marker

Procedure

1. Divide the contents of a can of soda equally among three identical glasses. Look into the glasses at eye level to make sure all of the glasses contain exactly the same amount of soda. You may need to pour the soda back and forth between the glasses until they all have exactly the same amount of soda. Since 12 ÷ 3 = 4, each glass now contains 4 ounces of soda.

2. Divide the contents of one of the glasses of soda in half by pouring exactly half of the soda from that glass into an empty glass. Each of these two glasses now contains 2 ounces of soda.

3. Pour half of the contents of one of the glasses containing 2 ounces of soda into an empty glass. Each of these two glasses now contains 1 ounce of soda.

4. Pour 1 ounce of soda from one of these glasses into the large glass. Use a marker to draw a horizontal line on the glass at the top of the soda. Write "1 ounce" next to the line.

5. Pour the other 1 ounce of soda into the large glass. Draw a horizontal line on the glass at the top of the soda. Write "2 ounces" next to the line. On the other side of the line write "¹/₄ cup." A cup is 8 ounces, so ¹/₄ cup is 2 ounces.

6. Take the remaining glass from step 2 containing 2 ounces of soda and divide the contents in half using one of the glasses you just emptied. Now each glass

contains 1 ounce. Pour 1 ounce of soda into the large glass, draw a horizontal line at the top of the soda, and write "3 ounces" next to the line.

7. Pour the other 1 ounce of soda into the large glass and draw a horizontal line at the top of the soda. Write "4 ounces" next to the line and "¹/₂ cup" on the other side of the line. Four ounces is ¹/₂ cup.

8. You have two glasses left with 4 ounces of soda in each. Divide the contents of one glass in half and each of these halves in half again, using the empty glasses. You now have four glasses of soda with 1 ounce of soda in each. (Keep the remaining 4 ounces for the Brain Stretcher activity.)

9. Add each of these ounces of soda to the marked glass one at a time. Draw lines at each addition and label them "5 ounces," "6 ounces," "7 ounces," and "8 ounces." Next to the 6-ounce line write "³⁄₄ cup." Next to the 8-ounce line write "1 cup."

10. You can use your measuring cup to measure the ingredients for a recipe.

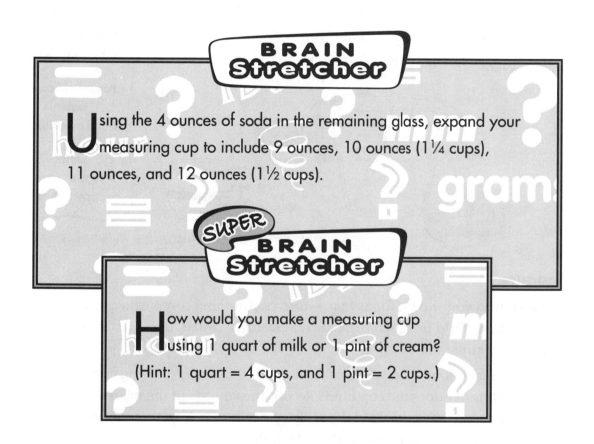

BRAIN Stretcher

Using the 4 ounces of soda in the remaining glass, expand your measuring cup to include 9 ounces, 10 ounces (1¼ cups), 11 ounces, and 12 ounces (1½ cups).

SUPER BRAIN Stretcher

How would you make a measuring cup using 1 quart of milk or 1 pint of cream? (Hint: 1 quart = 4 cups, and 1 pint = 2 cups.)

When Is a Cup Not a Cup?

Measure the cups around your house to see if any of them really are 1 cup.

Procedure

1. Look around your house for as many different drinking containers as you can find that could be called cups, such as teacups, coffee cups, plastic cups, paper cups, and so on.

2. Fill the first cup to the top with water and pour it into a measuring cup. How much water does the cup hold? Record the volume to the nearest ounce on a scrap of paper. Fold the scrap of paper in half so that the writing cannot be seen and tape it to the side of the cup.

3. Measure and label the remaining cups, and arrange them on a table.

4. Ask a friend or a family member to put the cups in a row from smallest to largest.

5. After your helper has put the cups in order, open the scraps of paper to see if he or she is correct.

6. Are any of your cups a true cup—exactly 8 ounces?

A Square Cup

Construct a square cup and learn to calculate the volume of various shapes.

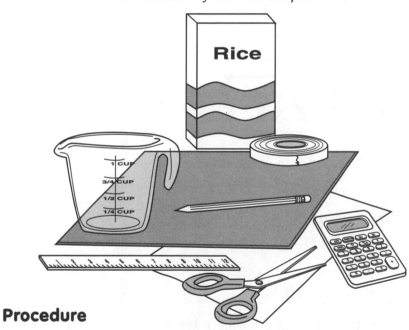

MATERIALS

1-cup measuring cup
pencil
cardboard
ruler
scissors
masking tape
uncooked rice
calculator
paper

Procedure

1. Looking at a measuring cup for reference, try to construct a cardboard cube that contains exactly 1 cup. Draw five squares that are exactly the same size on a piece of cardboard. Cut out the squares and tape them together to form a cube that is open on the top.

2. Measure a cup of rice using your square measuring cup. Pour the rice into an actual measuring cup. Does your cup measure a larger or smaller volume than an actual cup?

3. Construct a second square cup based on what you learned from constructing the first cup. Does this cup measure exactly 1 cup? Repeat step 2 to find out.

4. After you have constructed the perfect square cup, calculate the volume of your square cup in cubic inches. Measure the length, the width, and the height of your cup. Multiply all three numbers to find how many cubic inches are in 1 cup using a calculator if necessary. Record the volume on a sheet of paper.

5. How many cubic inches are there in 1 quart? To find out, multiply your answer in step 4 by 4, since there are 4 cups in 1 quart.

BRAIN Stretcher

How many cups are there in 1 cubic foot? Figure out how many cubic inches there are in 1 cubic foot, and divide this number by the number of cubic inches in 1 cup. To check your arithmetic, build a cube that measures 1 cubic foot (1 foot long by 1 foot wide by 1 foot tall) and fill it with soil, using a measuring cup. How many cups does it take to fill 1 cubic foot?

It's a Party

What if you wanted to cook something for a lot of friends, but the recipe only tells you how to make enough for half that many? Here's how to multiply a recipe.

Procedure

1. Copy the following chart on a piece of paper.

RECIPE INGREDIENTS

Ingredients	Original Recipe Amounts	Double the Amounts	Quadruple the Amounts

2. Find a recipe you would like to make for a party or a school bake sale, such as brownies, chocolate chip cookies, or cherry pie.

3. List the ingredients of the recipe in column 1 of the chart.

4. List the amounts of each ingredient of the recipe in column 2.

5. Double the amounts of the ingredients in column 2 and write the doubled amounts in column 3. Convert the amounts to larger units as necessary, using the Tips and Tricks box and a calculator if necessary. (For example, convert 8 tablespoons to ½ cup.)

6. Double the amounts of the ingredients in column 3 and write the quadrupled amounts in column 4. Convert the amounts to larger units as necessary.

7. How many people does your original recipe serve? How many people does the doubled recipe serve? How many people does the quadrupled recipe serve?

Tips and Tricks

3 teaspoons = 1 tablespoon

16 tablespoons = 1 cup

2 cups = 1 pint

2 pints = 1 quart

4 quarts = 1 gallon

Volume Addition

This game will help you practice converting between different English volumes.

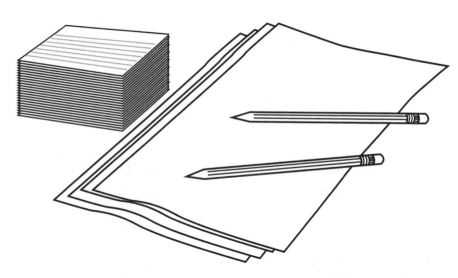

Game Preparation

Write one of the following expressions on each of 24 index cards.

1 teaspoon	$\frac{1}{2}$ cup	1 pint	3 quarts
3 teaspoons	$\frac{3}{4}$ cup	2 pints	4 quarts
1 tablespoon	1 cup	3 pints	1 gallon
8 tablespoons	2 cups	4 pints	2 gallons
$\frac{1}{8}$ cup	3 cups	1 quart	3 gallons
$\frac{1}{4}$ cup	4 cups	2 quarts	4 gallons

Game Rules

1. Shuffle the cards and place them facedown on the table.

2. Player 1 draws the top card from the deck and decides whether to keep this card or draw another. If the player decides to keep the first card, he or she places it facedown in front of himself or herself. If the player decides not to keep the first card, he or she places it facedown next to the deck (creating a discard pile) and draws another card. Player 1 must keep the second card.

3. Player 2 now draws the top card from the deck and decides whether to keep this card or draw another. If the player discards the first card, he or she must keep the second card.

4. Player 1 now draws another card. The process continues until each player has five cards.

5. Both players turn all their cards over and add the amounts on their cards together, converting all the amounts to the lowest common unit. Players may use the Tips and Tricks box and a pencil and paper. The player with the greatest total wins the round.

6. Return all the cards to the deck, shuffle the cards, and play another round. The first player to win three rounds is the winner.

Tips and Tricks ~~~~~

1 tablespoon = 3 teaspoons

1 cup = 16 tablespoons

1 pint = 2 cups

1 quart = 4 cups

1 gallon = 16 cups

Measuring Milliliters

Learn about liters, deciliters, centiliters, and milliliters by comparing them to English units of volume.

Procedure

1. Copy the following chart on a piece of paper.

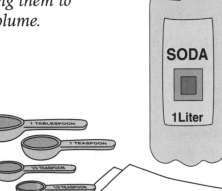

SODA

1Liter

ENGLISH TO METRIC CONVERSIONS

English Units	Number of English Units in 1 l	Number of Milliliters in English Unit
1 tablespoon		
1 teaspoon		
½ teaspoon		
¼ teaspoon		

2. There are 1,000 ml in 1 l. Does it take more or less than 1,000 table-spoons to fill a 1-l bottle?

    a. Fill an empty 1-l bottle with tablespoons of water. Have a friend help you keep track of the number of spoonfuls. Write the number of table-spoons in 1 l in column 2 of the chart.

    b. Convert the number of tablespoons in 1 l to the number of milliliters in 1 l. Divide by 1,000 by the number in column 2, using a calculator if necessary. Write the answer in column 3. Is 1 tablespoon larger or smaller than 1 ml?

3. Does it take more or less than 1,000 teaspoons to fill the bottle? Use a teaspoon to fill the bottle with water. Write the number of teaspoons in 1 l in column 2. Repeat step 2b to convert the number of teaspoons in 1 l to the number of milliliters in 1 l. Is 1 teaspoon larger or smaller than 1 ml?

4. Does it take more or less than 1,000 half teaspoons to fill the bottle? Fill the bottle with half teaspoons of water. Write the number of half tea-spoons in 1 l in column 2. Repeat step 2b to convert the number of half teaspoons in 1 l to the number of milliliters in 1 l. Is $\frac{1}{2}$ teaspoon larger or smaller than 1 ml?

5. Does it take more or less than 1,000 quarter teaspoons to fill the bottle? Fill the bottle with quarter teaspoons of water. Write the number of quarter teaspoons in 1 l in column 2. Repeat step 2b to convert the number of quarter teaspoons in 1 l to the number of milliliters in 1 l. Is $\frac{1}{4}$ teaspoon larger or smaller than 1 ml?

6. Now that you know the volume of 1 ml, you can determine the volume of other metric measurements, since they are all multiples of 10: 10 ml = 1 cl, 10 cl = 1 dl or 100 ml, 10 dl = 1 l or 1,000 ml.

Create a Liter Cube

*Make a liter cube and compare
its volume to volumes of English units.*

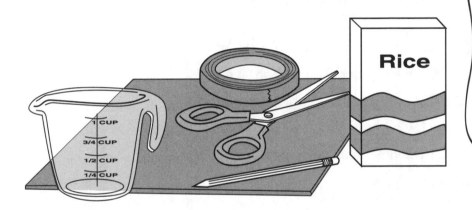

Procedure

1. Draw five squares on a piece of cardboard, making each square 10 cm by 10 cm. Cut out the squares.

2. Tape the five sides of the square together to make a cube that is open at the top. Tape all the edges so that the cube is sealed. Your cube holds exactly 1 l.

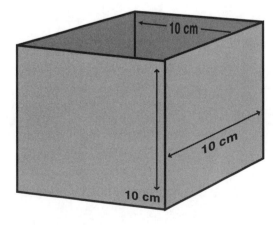

3. How does 1 l compare to English volume measurements? Take an English measuring cup and pour 1 cup of rice in the liter cube. Which is larger, 1 cup or 1 l? Add another cup of rice to the liter cube. You now have 2 cups of rice, or 1 pint. Which is larger, 1 pint or 1 l?

4. Add 2 more cups of rice to the liter cube. You now have a total of 4 cups, or 1 quart. Which is larger, 1 quart or 1 l?

BRAIN Stretcher

Since your liter cube is 10 cm wide, 10 cm long, and 10 cm high, it is $10 \times 10 \times 10$ or 1,000 cubic centimeters (cc). One cc is 1 cm by 1 cm by 1 cm. How many cubic centimeters are in a cubic meter?

The Price Is Right

Compare the prices of two grocery items when one price is for metric units and the other is for English units.

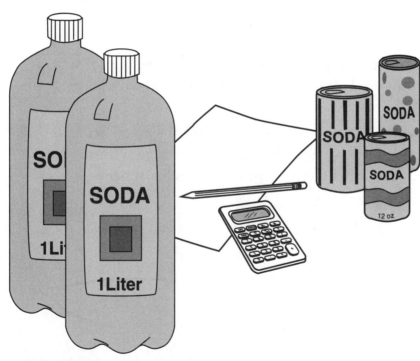

Procedure

1. Go to a supermarket and find bottles or cans of the same kind of soft drinks that are different sizes and prices. Write down the size and price of each item, such as one 2-l bottle of ginger ale for $2 and six 12-ounce cans of ginger ale for $2.95.

2. On another piece of paper, calculate the total volume of each product in ounces. You can use a calculator if necessary. For example, the total volume of six 12-ounce cans is 72 ounces, because 6 cans × 12 ounces per can = 72 ounces. To calculate the total volume of the 2-l bottle, first convert liters to ounces. Since 1 l equals 1.057 quarts, 2 l equals 2.114 quarts. One quart equals 32 ounces, so multiply 2.114 quarts by 32 ounces: 2.114 × 32 = 67.648. The total volume of the bottle is 67.6 ounces.

3. Now calculate the per ounce price of each product. To do this, divide the total cost by the total volume. For the canned soda, divide $2.95 by 72 ounces: $2.95 ÷ 72 = $0.04. The unit cost of the canned soda is 4¢ per ounce. For the bottled soda, divide $2 by 67.6 ounces: $2 ÷ 67.6 = $0.029. The unit cost of the bottled soda is 3¢ per ounce.

4. Rank the products from least expensive to most expensive per ounce. At 3¢ per ounce, the bottled soda is less expensive than the canned soda at 4¢ per ounce.

5. Show the original quantities and prices to a friend or family member and ask him or her to estimate how the products rank in order from least expensive to most expensive per ounce. How accurate is his or her estimated ranking?

~~~ IV ~~~

MEASURING WEIGHT IN ENGLISH AND METRIC UNITS

The English system of measuring weight is called "avoirdupois weight."

The avoirdupois system has eight different units of measurement, the most common of which are the ounce, the pound, and the ton. There are 16 ounces in 1 pound and 2,000 pounds in 1 ton. The avoirdupois system is used to measure everything except gems, precious metals such as gold and silver, and medicines. Gems and precious metals are weighed using "troy weight," in which the grain and the carat are common measurements. Medicines are weighed using what are called "apothecaries' measures."

COMMON ENGLISH UNITS OF WEIGHT (AVOIRDUPOIS UNITS)

English Unit	Abbreviation	English Equivalent
ounce	oz.	$\frac{1}{16}$ pound
pound	lb.	16 ounces
ton		2,000 pounds

Metric weights are measured in parts of a gram: milligrams, kilograms, and so on. As with the rest of the metric system, these units are based on multiples of 10: 1 g equals 1,000 mg, and 1 kg equals 1,000 g.

COMMON METRIC UNITS OF WEIGHT

Metric Unit	Abbreviation	Metric Equivalent
milligram	mg	0.001 g or 0.1 cg
centigram	cg	10 mg or .01 cg
gram	g	1,000 mg or 100 cg
kilogram	kg	1,000 g
metric ton	t	1,000 kg

In this section, you will learn to judge the weight of an object in ounces, pounds, and tons. You'll also get to know how to use metric units, and you'll compare English weight measurements to metric weight measurements.

CONVERSIONS FROM METRIC TO ENGLISH EQUIVALENTS

Metric Measurement	English Equivalent
1 g	0.0353 ounce
1 kg	2.2046 pounds
1 t	2,204.6 pounds (1.102 tons)

CONVERSIONS FROM ENGLISH TO METRIC EQUIVALENTS

English Measurement	Metric Equivalent
1 ounce	28.35 g
1 pound	0.454 kg or 454 g
1 ton	0.907 t

27

Outer Space

Weight is the result of the pull of gravity. The greater the pull of gravity, the more an object weighs. Each of the planets in our solar system has a weaker or stronger pull of gravity than Earth. How much would you weigh on the different planets?

MATERIALS

pencil
paper
calculator

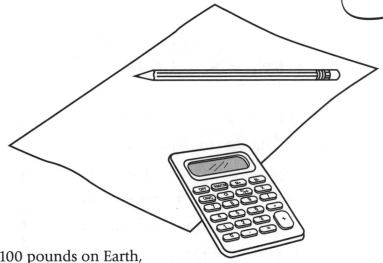

Procedure

1. If you weigh 100 pounds on Earth, here's what you would weigh on the other planets:

Mercury	37.8 pounds	Saturn	106.6 pounds
Venus	90.6 pounds	Uranus	90.5 pounds
Mars	37.9 pounds	Neptune	113.3 pounds
Jupiter	253.3 pounds	Pluto	6.7 pounds

2. Calculate your weight on each planet, using a pencil and paper, and a calculator if necessary. To determine your weight on

Mercury multiply your weight by 0.378
Venus multiply your weight by 0.906
Mars multiply your weight by 0.379
Jupiter multiply your weight by 2.533
Saturn multiply your weight by 1.066
Uranus multiply your weight by 0.905
Neptune multiply your weight by 1.133
Pluto multiply your weight by 0.067

BRAIN Stretcher

The less you weigh, the higher you can jump. When U.S. astronauts landed on the Moon, they found they weighed only one-sixth their weight on Earth and could jump six times as high. How high can you jump on Earth? How high could you jump on the Moon?

28

One Ounce

How much is an ounce?

MATERIALS

**2 pencils
paper
bottle cap
paper clip
slice of apple
quarter
25 pennies
stick of butter
butter knife
masking tape
2 paper cups
ruler**

Procedure

1. Copy the following chart on a piece of paper.

ITEM WEIGHTS

Item	Weight (More or Less Than 1 Ounce)
bottle cap	
paper clip	
slice of apple	
quarter	
25 pennies	
_____ pennies	exactly 1 ounce

2. Find the following items: a bottle cap, a paper clip, a slice of apple, a quarter, and 25 pennies. List the items you found in column 1 of the chart.

3. Take a stick of butter from the refrigerator. A pound of butter contains four sticks of butter. Since 1 pound of butter is 16 ounces, each stick of butter weighs exactly 4 ounces. Cut the stick of butter into four equal pieces. Each piece of butter weighs exactly 1 ounce. Keep one 1-ounce piece of butter and put the rest back in the refrigerator.

4. Construct a scale by taping a paper cup to each end of a ruler. Lay the center of the ruler across a pencil or your finger so that the ruler balances.

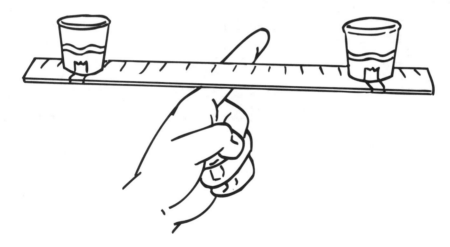

5. Place the 1-ounce piece of butter in one of the paper cups.

6. Place each item in turn, in the other cup to determine which of these items weighs less and which weighs more than 1 ounce. Write the results in column 2 of your chart. Do any items weigh exactly 1 ounce? Does a specific number of pennies weigh exactly 1 ounce?

One Pound

What does a pound of something feel like?

MATERIALS

1-pound package of any food (such as butter, flour, or spaghetti)

15 other packaged foods of different weight

masking tape

2 players

Game Rules

1. Place something that weighs exactly 1 pound, such as a 1-pound package of butter, flour, or spaghetti, on the kitchen table or countertop.

2. Player 1 leaves the room. Player 2 stays in the kitchen and finds five other packaged food items that weigh more than 1 pound, less than 1 pound, and exactly 1 pound, using the Tips and Tricks box for help. Player 2 covers their weights with masking tape and places the packages on the table next to the 1-pound package.

3. Player 2 asks player 1 to return to the room. Player 1 has to guess whether each of the five items weighs more than 1 pound, less than 1 pound, or exactly 1 pound. Player 1 earns 1 point for each item guessed correctly.

4. The players switch places, with Player 1 placing five new items on the table and player 2 guessing their relative weights. The first player to earn 11 points wins the game.

SUPER ONE POUND

Instead of guessing whether an item weighs more than, less than, or exactly 1 pound, players put the five items in order from lightest to heaviest. Players earn 1 point for each item that is in the correct order.

Tips and Tricks

- ● A pound is exactly 16 ounces, so if a food item weighs less than 16 ounces, it weighs less than 1 pound. If it weighs more than 16 ounces, it weighs more than 1 pound.

- ● A pound is about 454 g. So if a food item weighs less than 454 g, it weighs less than 1 pound. If it weighs more than 454 g, it weighs more than 1 pound.

Estimating Weights

Practice estimating the weight of yourself, your pet, a younger sibling, and various household items in pounds and kilograms.

MATERIALS

pencil

several pieces of paper

various household items

bathroom scale

calculator

Procedure

1. Copy the following chart on a piece of paper.

ESTIMATED AND ACTUAL WEIGHTS

Items to Weigh	Guessed Weight in Pounds	Actual Weight in Pounds	Guessed Weight in Kilograms	Actual Weight in Kilograms
yourself				
your pet				
younger sibling (age: _____)				
backpack full of books				
kitchen chair				
bowl of fruit				
lamp				
your sneakers				
empty suitcase				
pot of water				
object of your choice				

2. Collect as many of the items listed in the chart as you can.

3. Guess your weight in pounds. Then weigh yourself on the bathroom scale to get your actual weight. Write your guessed weight and your actual weight in columns 2 and 3 of the chart.

4. Pick up one of the items on the list, such as your pet. Guess how much your pet weighs in pounds. Write your pet's guessed weight in column 2.

5. Get on the scale holding your pet. What do you and your pet together weigh? Subtract your weight from the combined weight. The difference is the weight of your pet. Write your pet's actual weight in column 3.

6. Guess how much your pet weighs in kilograms. Write the guessed weight in kilograms in column 4 of the chart.

7. To find the actual weight of your pet in kilograms, divide the weight in column 3 by 2.2, using a calculator if necessary. Write the actual weight in kilograms in column 5.

8. Repeat steps 4 to 7 to weigh the other items on the list.

BRAIN Stretcher

Find two items that weigh approximately the same amount but are different in size and shape. Which item weighs more: 1 pound of feathers or 1 pound of lead? Which item has a greater volume?

Guess and Weigh

Play Guess and Weigh with a friend to practice estimating the weight of objects.

MATERIALS

100 pennies or poker chips

household objects weighing more than 1 pound

2 pencils

2 pieces of paper

bathroom scale

2 players

Game Rules

1. Give each player 25 pennies or poker chips. The bank keeps the rest of the pennies.

2. Player 1 chooses an object from around the house to weigh.

3. Both players secretly write down how much they think the object weighs, then bet one to five pennies on their guess.

4. Players take turns weighing the object by weighing themselves holding the object on a bathroom scale, weighing themselves without the object, and subtracting their weight from the combined weight.

5. Players reveal their guesses. The player who comes closest to the actual weight without going over it wins the round. The winning player keeps the pennies he or she bet, and takes an equal amount from the bank. The losing player gives the pennies he or she bet to the bank.

6. Player 2 chooses an object to be weighed and the game continues. The player with the most pennies after 10 rounds wins the game. If a player loses all his or her pennies before 10 rounds, the game is over.

32

One Ton

We've all used the expression "That weighs a ton," but how much is a ton? Learn the relative weight of large animals, in tons and metric tons.

MATERIALS

pencil
paper
encyclopedia
calculator

Procedure

1. Copy the following chart on a piece of paper.

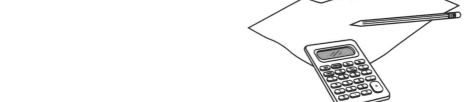

AVERAGE ANIMAL WEIGHTS

Animals	Weight in Pounds	Weight in Kilograms	Weight in Tons	Weight in Metric Tons
elephant				
blue whale				
hippopotamus				
Tyrannosaurus rex				
rhinoceros				
gorilla				
horse				
giraffe				

2. Using an encyclopedia, look up the average weight of each animal listed in column 1 of the chart, starting with the elephant. If the weight is given in pounds, write the weight in column 2. If the weight is given in kilograms, write the weight in column 3. If the weight is given in tons, write the weight in column 4. If the weight is given in metric tons, write the weight in column 5.

3. Calculate the missing weights in pounds, kilograms, tons, or metric tons for each animal, and write these weights in the columns. Use the Tips and Tricks box for help in converting, and a calculator if necessary.

4. Rank the animals from heaviest to lightest. Which animal weighs closest to 1 ton? Which weighs closest to 1 metric ton?

5. Is there any combination of animals on the list that together would weigh 1 ton? Are there any that would weigh 1 metric ton?

Tips and Tricks

To convert pounds

    to kilograms multiply by 0.454

    to tons divide by 2,000

To convert kilograms

    to pounds multiply by 2.2046

    to metric tons divide by 1,000

To convert tons

    to pounds multiply by 2,000

To convert metric tons

    to kilograms multiply by 1,000

Grams and Milligrams

33

Search for examples of metric weight measurements and convert them to pounds and ounces.

MATERIALS

pencil

paper

various packaged household items weighed in milligrams, grams, or kilograms

calculator

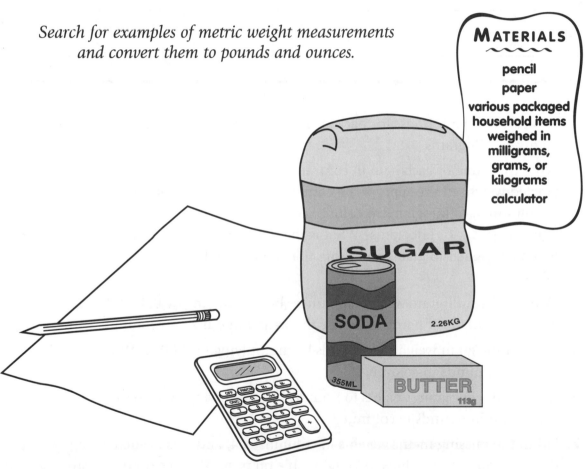

Procedure

1. Copy the following chart on a piece of paper.

ITEM WEIGHTS

Household Items	Weight in Milligrams	Weight in Ounces	Weight in Grams	Weight in Pounds	Weight in Kilograms

2. Look around your house for packaged items weighed in milligrams, grams, or kilograms.

3. Write the name of each item in column 1 of the chart and write the labeled weight in the appropriate column: milligrams in column 2, grams in column 4, or kilograms in column 6. Are more items weighed in milligrams, grams, or kilograms? What is the difference between the items that are weighed in grams and those that are weighed in milligrams or kilograms?

4. Convert the milligram weights to ounces by multiplying by 0.0000353, using a calculator if necessary. Write the weight in ounces in column 3.

5. Convert the gram weights to pounds by multiplying by 0.0022. Write the weight in pounds in column 5.

6. Convert the kilogram weights to pounds by multiplying by 2.2046. Write the weight in pounds in column 5.

7. Fill in the missing metric weights in columns 2, 4, and 6 as needed, using the Common Metric Units of Weight table on page 74 if necessary to convert between metric units.

V

Measuring Temperature in Degrees Fahrenheit and Celsius

In the early eighteenth century, two scientists invented different scales for measuring temperature. Both scientists based their scales on the freezing and boiling points of water. German physicist Gabriel Daniel Fahrenheit (1686–1736) called his temperature scale the Fahrenheit scale and set the freezing point of water at 32°F and the boiling point of water at 212°F. On the Fahrenheit scale, 0°F is the lowest temperature of a mixture of equal weights of salt and snow.

Swedish astronomer Anders Celsius (1701–1744) called his temperature scale the Celsius scale and set the freezing point of water at 0°C and the boiling point at 100°C. The Fahrenheit scale is used in the United States, while the Celsius scale (also known as the centigrade scale) is used in the rest of the world.

In this section, you'll practice measuring temperature in both degrees Celsius and Fahrenheit and learn the difference between the two scales. You'll also learn how to convert temperature from degrees Fahrenheit to Celsius and from degrees Celsius to Fahrenheit.

34

Water, Water Everywhere

Learn common temperatures in Fahrenheit and Celsius using a thermometer.

MATERIALS

pencil

several pieces of paper

Fahrenheit and Celsius thermometers, or one that shows both scales

8 drinking glasses

water

timer

ice

English measuring-spoon set

table salt

teacup or mug

tea bag

calculator

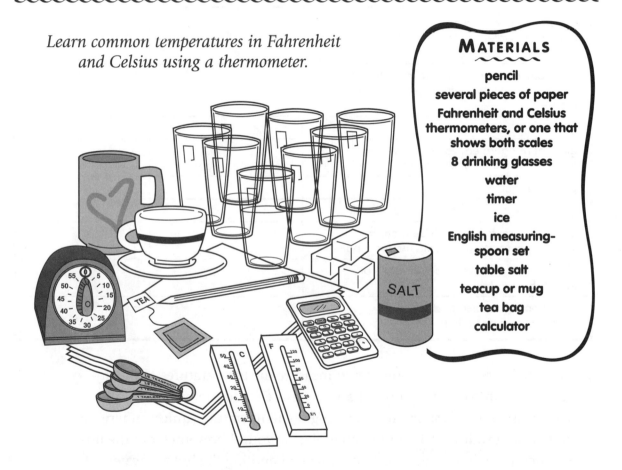

Procedure

1. Copy the following chart on a piece of paper.

TEMPERATURES OF LIQUIDS

Liquids	Temperature in Degrees Fahrenheit	Temperature in Degrees Celsius
glass of cold tap water (Use only the cold faucet and let the water run for 1 minute before filling the glass.)		
glass of ice water (Leave the ice in the glass for at least 15 minutes before measuring the temperature.)		
glass of ice		
glass of refrigerated water (Use water that's been in the refrigerator for 1 hour.)		
glass of room temperature water		
glass of ice water with 1 teaspoon of salt		
glass of warm tap water (Use water the same temperature you would use for a bath.)		
glass of hot tap water (Use only the hot faucet. Be careful!)		
cup of hot tea cooled to drinking temperature (Be careful!)		

2. Use the Fahrenheit thermometer to measure the temperatures of the liquids listed in column 1 of the chart. To ensure an accurate reading, fill each glass or cup just before measuring the temperature (unless otherwise noted) and wait 2 or 3 minutes after placing your thermometer in the liquid before taking it out. Use caution when handling the hot tap water and hot tea. Write the temperature in degrees Fahrenheit in column 2 of the chart.

3. Based on your results, answer the following questions:

   a. Which is colder, a glass of ice water or a glass of refrigerated water?

   b. Which is colder, salted ice water or plain ice water?

   c. Which is hotter, tea that feels warm to your mouth or a bath that feels warm to your touch?

4. Convert each of the temperatures from Fahrenheit to Celsius and write the temperature in degrees Celsius in column 3. Use the following formula, and a calculator if necessary.

$$\frac{5\,(°F - 32)}{9} = °C$$

First subtract 32 from the Fahrenheit temperature. Multiply the difference by 5, then divide the product by 9. The answer is the temperature in degrees Celsius. For example, to convert 50°F to degrees Celsius:

$$50 - 32 = 18$$
$$18 \times 5 = 90$$
$$90 \div 9 = 10$$

So 50°F is equivalent to 10°C.

5. Confirm the answers from step 4 by measuring the temperature of each liquid again, this time with a Celsius thermometer.

What's the Temperature?

This lively game helps you practice recognizing temperatures in degrees Celsius and Fahrenheit.

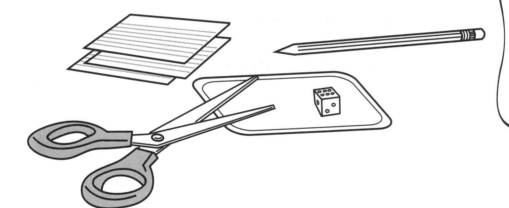

MATERIALS

scissors

self-adhesive label

die

pencil

18 index cards

2 players

Game Preparation

1. Cut the self-adhesive label into six squares, each about the size of one face of the die. Stick the squares on the faces of the die. On each of three squares, write an "F," which stands for Fahrenheit. On each of the other three squares, write a "C," which stands for Celsius.

2. Write one of the following statements on each of eight index cards. (Notice that the expressions do not indicate whether the temperature is in degrees Celsius or Fahrenheit.)

> Water boils at 100°
> Water boils at 212°
> Water freezes at 0°

Water freezes at 32°

A warm sunny day in Florida is 25°

You'd probably wear a sweater if it was 50°

You bake a cake at 375°

You are going ice-skating and it's 20°

3. Each player then makes up five of his or her own statements similar to these and writes each on an index card. As before, do not state whether the temperature is in degrees Celsius or Fahrenheit.

Game Rules

1. Shuffle all the cards and place them facedown in a stack in the center of the table.

2. Player 1 rolls the Celsius-Fahrenheit die. The letter that lands faceup determines the temperature scale that will be used in this round. Players try to be the first to slap any card turned over that is a correct statement with a temperature in degrees Celsius if a C is rolled or in degrees Fahrenheit if an F is rolled.

3. Players take turns turning over the top card and placing it faceup in a pile. The first player to slap a faceup card with a correct statement wins all the faceup cards. If the player slaps a card that is incorrect, then he or she has to give any cards he or she has won to the other player.

4. The first player to win all the cards wins the round.

5. Player 2 rolls the die and another round is played. The first player to win three rounds wins the game.

BRAIN Stretchers

1. To convert temperature from degrees Fahrenheit to Celsius, use the following formula:

$$\frac{5\,(°F - 32)}{9} = °C$$

(See page 97 for an example.)

2. To convert temperature from degrees Celsius to Fahrenheit, use the following formula:

$$\frac{(°C \times 9)}{5} + 32 = °F$$

For example, what is 20°C in degrees Fahrenheit?

$$20 \times 9 = 180$$

$$180 \div 5 = 36$$

$$36 + 32 = 68$$

So 20°C is equivalent to 68°F.

VI

MEASURING TIME

Our measurement of time is based on the movement of Earth around the Sun and of the Moon around Earth. Time is measured in seconds, minutes, hours, days, weeks, months, years, decades, centuries, and millennia. There are 60 seconds in a minute, 60 minutes in an hour, 24 hours in a day, 7 days in a week, approximately 4 weeks in a month, 12 months in a year, 10 years in a decade, 100 years in a century, and 1,000 years in a millennium.

In this section, you will learn how to determine the length of a second, use a candle to measure time, construct a sundial, and figure out the time in different time zones. By the end of this section, you'll know so much about all kinds of measurement that you'll be a measurement master.

Ten Times!

What can you do in 1 second?

Game Preparation

Copy the chart on the next page on a piece of paper.

GAME RESULTS

Task	Player 1 10 Task Time	Player 2 10 Task Time	Player 1 One Task Time	Player 2 One Task Time
snapping fingers				
clapping hands				
hopping				
saying player's own name				
counting "one Mississippi . . ."				
saying "good morning"				
climbing a flight of stairs				

Game Rules

1. Player 2 starts the stopwatch and player 1 performs the first task listed in column 1 of the chart, snapping his or her fingers 10 times as fast as possible. On the tenth snap, player 1 shouts, "Done!" and player 2 stops the stopwatch. Player 1's time is entered in column 2 of the chart.

2. Player 2 then snaps his or her fingers 10 times as fast as possible while player 1 times the task. Player 2's time is entered in column 3 of the chart.

3. Players take turns performing each of the remaining tasks 10 times while the other player times the task.

4. When all of the tasks have been performed, player 1 divides each of his or her times in column 2 by 10 to find the time it took him or her to do each task once. Players can use a calculator if necessary. Player 1 writes the one task time in column 4.

5. Player 2 then divides each of his or her times in column 3 by 10 to find the time it took him or her to do each task. Player 2 writes his or her task time in column 5.

6. Which player did which task the fastest? Which tasks took less than a second? Which tasks took more than a second? Did any tasks take exactly 1 second?

BRAIN Stretchers

1. Try to find a task that you can complete or an expression you can say 10 times in exactly 10 seconds. If you can complete a task exactly 10 times in 10 seconds, then it takes you exactly 1 second to do the task once.

2. Once you know how long a second is, try to judge how long a minute is. Say or do something that you think takes 1 second to do once. Then do it 60 times. Time yourself to see if it really takes 1 minute.

3. How many seconds are in an hour? What is 60×60?

4. How many seconds are in a day? What is $60 \times 60 \times 24$?

5. How many seconds are in a week? What is $60 \times 60 \times 24 \times 7$?

6. How many seconds are in the month of April? What is $60 \times 60 \times 24 \times 30$?

7. How many seconds are in a year? What is $60 \times 60 \times 24 \times 365$?

8. How many days do a million seconds make? What is $1,000,000 \div (60 \times 60 \times 24)$?

How long does it take to drink 1 ounce of water? Measure out 1 cup (8 ounces) of water. Time how long it takes you to drink the water, and divide your time by 8 to find out how long it takes you to drink 1 ounce of water. Time how long it takes to drink a 12-ounce can of soda and divide your time by 12. Can you drink a 12-ounce can of soda at the same rate you can drink an 8-ounce glass of water?

Candle Hour Power

Before there were mechanical clocks, people sometimes used candles to tell time. Here's how you can, too.

MATERIALS

ruler

tall, thin candle with the same diameter at the top as at the bottom (requires adult help)

pencil

paper

candleholder

plate

watch or clock

marker

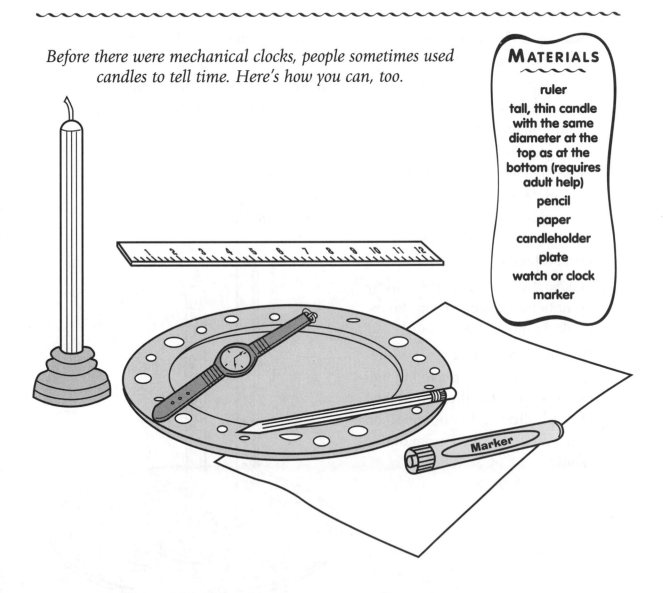

Procedure

1. Measure the length of the candle. Record the length on a piece of paper.

2. Place the candle in a candleholder. Make sure there is a plate under the candleholder so that you don't get wax on the table.

3. Have an adult light the candle.

4. Exactly 1 hour later, blow out the candle. Never leave a lit candle in a room by itself. Either you or your adult helper should stay in the room while the candle is lit.

5. When the candle has cooled, take it out of the holder and measure the length of the candle. Subtract this length from the original length to determine how much of the candle burned in 1 hour.

6. Starting at the top of the candle, use the length determined in step 5 to mark the rest of the candle in 1-hour segments. Mark completely around the candle. For example, if the candle burned 1 inch (2.5 cm) in 1 hour, you would draw the first line 1 inch (2.5 cm) from the top, the second line 1 inch (2.5 cm) below the first, and so on.

7. Make a thinner line at the halfway point between each of your hour marks to indicate half hours.

8. Use the marker to write a 1 at the first thick line from the top to indicate 1 hour, a 2 at the second thick line to indicate 2 hours, and so on until you get to the bottom of the candle.

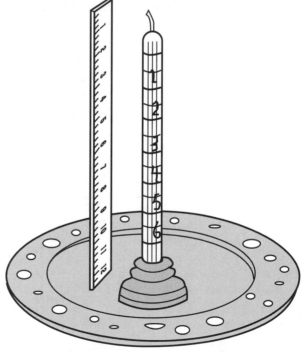

BRAIN Stretcher

Lots of things can be used to measure time. Ask an adult to punch a hole in the lid of a large empty jar, such as a mayonnaise jar. Fill the jar with sand and secure the lid on the jar. Hold the jar upside down over a bowl and ask a friend to start a stopwatch. How long does it take the sand to empty out of the jar? If it takes 30 minutes, you made a 30-minute timer. Write "30 minutes" on the jar. Experiment with different size jars and holes of different diameters to make timers of different duration.

Create a Sundial

*Make a sundial on a sunny
day and test your sundial's accuracy.*

MATERIALS

pencil

poster board or
cardboard

large round plate

ruler

dowel or yard-
stick

8 toothpicks

clock or watch

marker

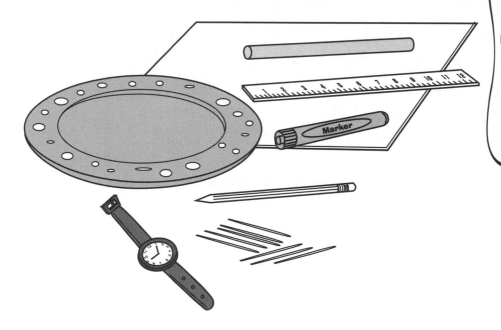

Procedure

1. Using a pencil, draw a circle on a sheet of poster board by tracing around a large round plate. Mark the center of the circle, using a ruler to find the center.

2. Place the poster board outside on the ground in a place that is sunny all day.

3. Make a hole in the center of the circle and insert a dowel or yardstick in the hole. Press the dowel into the ground so that it stands straight up in the middle of the circle.

4. Stick eight toothpicks in the ground to mark the position of the poster board. Place a toothpick at each of the corners and in the middle of each side.

5. Every hour on the hour, use the ruler and a marker to mark the position of the shadow of the dowel on the circle. Indicate the hour next to this mark. Mark as many hours as you can.

6. Leave your sundial outside and use it to tell time. If it is going to rain, bring your sundial inside, but leave your toothpick markers in place so you can return the sundial to its original position.

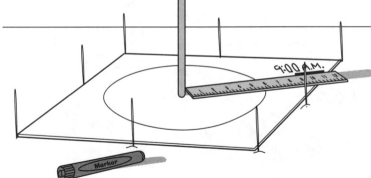

7. Approximately 1 week later, check the time on the sundial against the time on your watch. Is the sundial still accurate? If it is not accurate, how much has the time changed?

8. Check the time again approximately 2 weeks later. Can you figure out why a sundial is accurate for only a few days?

Clock Search

*Search for clocks around your house
and learn about the different types of clocks.*

Procedure

1. Have everyone in your family (including yourself) guess the number of clocks that are in your house and make a list. All guesses should be kept secret. Have everyone write their names on their lists, fold their lists, and place them in a brown paper bag.

2. Go around the house and look for clocks. Create a master list of all the clocks in your house. Count not only clock radios, alarm clocks, and watches but also the clocks built in to your computer, stove, microwave, or VCR.

3. Next to each clock on the list, write whether the clock is analog (has a dial) or digital. Note whether the clock indicates seconds. Also note whether the clock indicates A.M. and P.M.

4. After your clock hunt, open the guess lists in the brown paper bag. Whose guess is closest to the actual number of clocks in your house?

5. Group your clocks by type.

How many analog clocks do you have?
How many digital clocks do you have?
How many clocks have second hands or indicate seconds?
How many clocks indicate A.M. and P.M.?

BRAIN Stretcher

The abbreviations A.M. and P.M. come from Latin. The abbreviation a.m. stands for *ante meridiem* and means "before midday," and p.m. stands for *post meridiem* and means "after midday."

The military uses a 24-hour clock, with 1:00 A.M. being 0100 hours (which is read as oh–one hundred hours). Noon is 1200 hours (twelve hundred hours). After noon, everything really changes, since you keep counting from 12 rather than start all over at 1 again. So 1:00 P.M. is 1300 hours (thirteen hundred hours), and midnight is 2400 hours (twenty-four hundred hours). Likewise, 3:00 A.M. is 0300 hours (oh–three hundred hours), while 3:00 P.M. is 1500 hours (fifteen hundred hours).

All Over the United States

What are kids all over the United States doing when you are eating your breakfast or getting out of school? Learn about time zones and you'll have a pretty good idea.

MATERIALS

pencil
paper
atlas, phone book, or organizer

Procedure

1. Copy the following chart on a piece of paper.

2. Think about your daily schedule. What time do you wake up? Go to school? Have math class? Eat lunch? What time do you leave school? Eat dinner? Go to bed? Write these times in column 2 of the chart.

LOCAL TIMES

	Your Time	New York Time	Chicago Time	Denver Time	San Francisco Time	Anchorage Time	Honolulu Time
wake up							
go to school							
eat lunch							
have math class							
leave school							
eat dinner							
go to bed							

3. Use a time zone map (from an atlas, phone book, or organizer) to find the time in New York, Chicago, Denver, San Francisco, Anchorage, and Honolulu when you wake up. (If you live in one of these cities, choose another city in the same time zone for your chart.) Write these times in the appropriate columns of the chart.

4. Fill in the rest of your chart using the time zone map.

5. What do you think children in these other cities are doing when you are eating lunch? Or when you're going to bed?

1. Draw or trace a map of the United States. Shade each of the time zones.
2. Label the cities on your map where relatives or friends live. What is the difference in time between where your relatives live and where you live? If you live in New York, why might it be a bad idea to call your cousin in San Francisco at 8:00 A.M. your time?

Use an atlas to determine the distance in miles (kilometers) from your house to each of your relatives' houses. Which of your relatives lives the farthest from you? For which of your relatives is the time difference between you the greatest? Are time zones related only to distance? What else is a factor?

MEASUREMENT MASTER CERTIFICATE

Now that you've mastered all the measurement facts, problems, and games in this book, you are officially certified as a measurement master! Make a photocopy of this certificate, write your name on the copy, and hang it on the wall.

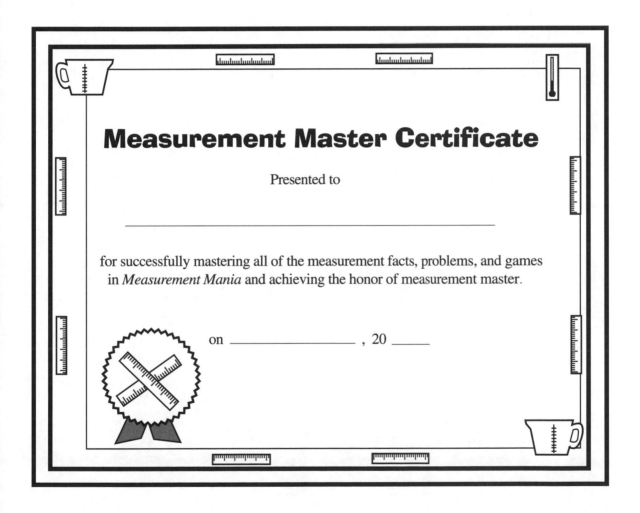

Measurement Master Certificate

Presented to

_____

for successfully mastering all of the measurement facts, problems, and games in *Measurement Mania* and achieving the honor of measurement master.

on _____ , 20 _____

Index